Date: 7/19/18

ANGRY earth

BLINDING BLIZZARDS

By Michael Portman

Gareth Stevens
Publishing

Please visit our website, www.garethstevens.com. For a free color catalog of all our high-quality books, call toll free 1-800-542-2595 or fax 1-877-542-2596.

Library of Congress Cataloging-in-Publication Data

Portman, Michael, 1976-
Blinding blizzards / Michael Portman.
    p. cm. — (Angry Earth)
Includes index.
ISBN 978-1-4339-6531-9 (pbk.)
ISBN 978-1-4339-6532-6 (6-pack)
ISBN 978-1-4339-6529-6 (library binding)
1. Blizzards—Juvenile literature. I. Title.
QC926.37.P67 2012
551.55'5—dc23

                                            2011022848

First Edition

Published in 2012 by
Gareth Stevens Publishing
111 East 14th Street, Suite 349
New York, NY 10003

Copyright © 2012 Gareth Stevens Publishing

Designer: Katelyn E. Reynolds
Editor: Therese Shea

Photo credits: Cover, pp. 1, 26–27, 29 (inset), (pp. 3–32 text/image box graphics) iStockphoto.com; (cover, pp. 1, 3–32 background and newspaper graphics) Shutterstock.com; p. 4 Herbert A. French/ Buyenlarge/Getty Images; p. 5 Wallace G. Levison/Dahlstrom Collection/Time Life Pictures/Getty Images; p. 6 Buyenlarge/Getty Images; p. 7 Hulton Archive/Getty Images; pp. 8, 10, 25 (inset) Thinkstock.com; pp. 9, 15, 26 Scott Olson/Getty Images; p. 11 Herbert/Archive Photos/Getty Images; p. 12 Chip Somodevilla/Getty Images; pp. 12–13 Josh Coleman/Getty Images; p. 14 Devendra M. Singh/AFP/Getty Images; p. 16 Seymour Hewitt/Iconica/Getty Images; p. 17 Dorling Kindersley/ Getty Images; pp. 18–21 Buffalo State College_Courier-Express_Collection; p. 22 Tim Clary/AFP/Getty Images; p. 23 NASA; p. 25 (main) NOAA via Getty Images; p. 28 Adem Altan/AFP/Getty Images; p. 29 (main) Alan Shortall/Workbook Stock/Getty Images.

Printed in the United States of America

CPSIA compliance information: Batch #CW12GS: For further information contact Gareth Stevens, New York, New York at 1-800-542-2595.

CONTENTS

Words in the glossary appear in **bold** type the first time they are used in the text.

THE GREAT WHITE HURRICANE

March 1888 began with unusually warm temperatures along the East Coast of the United States. However, on March 12, temperatures dropped. The warm rain started to freeze, and the wind began to howl. By midnight, the rain had turned into snow.

For almost 2 days, snow and wind continued nonstop. By the time the storm ended, between 40 and 50 inches (102 and 127 cm) of snow had fallen in many places. Major cities, including New York and Boston, were at a standstill. The Blizzard of 1888, often called the "Great White **Hurricane**," is one of the most famous storms in American history.

streetcar in Washington, DC, in March 1888

Walloping Winds

During the 1888 storm, wind speeds exceeded 60 miles (97 km) per hour. **Gusts** of over 80 miles (129 km) per hour were reported on Long Island, New York. The winds and falling snow erased footprints in less than 5 minutes.

◁ A person walks on the Brooklyn Bridge in New York City after the Blizzard of 1888. Trains and cars couldn't cross it.

6

Horse-drawn carts carry snow to the East River in New York City after the Blizzard of 1888.

The strong winds of the 1888 storm snapped **telegraph** and telephone wires, and snow blocked roads and railways. In some areas, the heavy winds created **snowdrifts** 50 feet (15 m) high! Trains were either stopped or took hours to travel just a few miles. In New York City, people climbed down from a stuck elevated train using ladders.

Some people tried to melt the mounds of snow by setting fires. Fires that got out of control did great **damage** to buildings since firefighters couldn't respond quickly. In the end, more than 400 people died as a result of the Great White Hurricane.

A New Way to Move

The Blizzard of 1888 led to the creation of the New York City subway, an underground railway system. Trains on ground tracks and those that were elevated had been useless during the blizzard. The New York subway began operating in 1904.

WHAT IS A BLIZZARD?

According to the US National Weather Service (NWS), a blizzard is a storm that lasts at least 3 hours and includes large amounts of falling or blowing snow. Blizzard winds are faster than 35 miles (56 km) per hour, and visibility is less than 1/4 mile (0.4 km). A severe blizzard is one with temperatures below 10°F (–12°C), winds above 45 miles (72 km) per hour, and visibility near zero.

The word "blizzard" originally meant a large amount of gunfire. In the 1870s, a newspaper in Iowa used the word "blizzard" to describe a snowstorm. Soon, "blizzard" became the common term for a major snowstorm.

slow-traveling cars in a blizzard

No Falling Snow Needed

Not all snowstorms are blizzards. And not all blizzards are accompanied by falling snow. Sometimes strong winds blow around snow that has already fallen, creating a blizzard. The blowing snow causes the same blinding, unsafe conditions as falling snow.

◁ A woman walks in low visibility during a 2011 blizzard in Chicago, Illinois. The storm dropped the third-largest amount of snow the city has ever had at one time.

HOW DOES SNOW FORM?

All air contains **water vapor**. When air rises into the upper atmosphere, it cools. The water vapor begins to change into tiny drops of water that collect around bits of dust. Water drops and dust are what clouds are made of. As the temperature in the cloud dips several degrees below freezing, the small water drops turn into tiny ice crystals. These ice crystals stick together until they form snowflakes.

When snowflakes get bigger, they become heavier and fall out of the clouds. If the air gets warmer as the snowflakes fall, they melt and turn into rain. If the air stays cold, the snowflakes fall to the ground as snow.

Weird Weather

It's possible for snow to fall on a mountaintop while it's warm, raining, or even sunny in a valley below. This is because the air at the top of the mountain is much colder than the air in the valley.

These are snowflakes as they look under a microscope. Different temperatures affect the shape of the crystals.

DANGEROUS SNOW

It only takes a little snow to create problems in cities and towns, especially in places where snowfall is uncommon. Blizzards make these problems add up quickly. Strong winds can turn powdery snow into a **whiteout**, making it hard to see. Whiteouts, along with snowdrifts, make traveling by car or airplane unsafe and sometimes impossible.

Heavy, wet snow can weigh down roofs of buildings, causing them to cave in. Strong winds and heavy snow can break tree limbs and power lines. The **extreme** cold temperatures that accompany blizzards can also make water pipes freeze or burst.

Blizzards make traveling by car unsafe and many times can lead to serious accidents.
▽

Snow and Water

Different types of snow contain different amounts of water. The amount of water in 10 inches (25 cm) of snow can range from less than an inch (2.5 cm) to as much as 3 inches (7.6 cm). Generally, the colder the air temperature and ground temperature, the drier the snow will be.

WINDCHILL WARNINGS

Strong winds can make the air temperature feel much colder than it actually is. This is called windchill. For instance, a wind that's 35 miles (56 km) per hour combined with a temperature of 30°F (–1°C) can feel like 14°F (–10°C).

People exposed to extremely low windchill temperatures face the danger of frostbite. Frostbite occurs when skin or cells beneath the skin freeze. Frostbite can cause lasting damage. In extreme cases, it can result in the loss of the affected body parts.

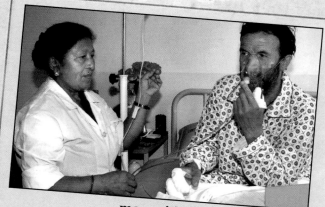

man with frostbitten fingers

Signs of Frostbite

- cold, burning, painful, or itchy skin
- loss of feeling, especially in fingers, toes, ears, nose, or chin
- pale or white appearance in areas exposed to extreme cold

Treatments

- soak frostbitten areas in warm water
- don't rub frostbitten body parts or expose them to direct heat, such as stoves, fireplaces, or heating pads
- seek medical attention as soon as possible

◁ In cold temperatures, the best way to fight frostbite is to cover as much skin as possible and spend little time outside.

15

Drinking warm liquids in cold weather can help maintain a healthy body temperature and prevent hypothermia.

Another danger of windchill is hypothermia. This occurs when the body loses heat faster than it can produce it. Cold wind can reduce body heat very quickly. Normally, body temperature is around 98.6°F (37°C). Hypothermia causes body temperature to drop below 95°F (35°C). As the body cools, the heart, lungs, and other organs stop working properly. If left untreated, hypothermia can lead to death.

Children and the elderly are at greater risk for hypothermia. Children lose heat faster than adults. The elderly may suffer from medical conditions that make it harder for their bodies to produce heat.

Signs of Hypothermia

• uncontrollable shivering
• confusion
• trouble speaking and moving
• sleepiness or lack of energy

Treatments

• move to a warm location

• remove wet clothing

• warm the center of the body first, not the arms or legs

• drink warm liquids

• seek medical attention as soon as possible

THE BLIZZARD OF '77

The Blizzard of '77 is the most famous blizzard in the history of Buffalo, New York. The winter of 1976 to 1977 had been especially bitter. Snow that had fallen throughout November, December, and January never had a chance to melt.

January 28, 1977, started out as a calm, mild day. Overnight, the temperature had risen to 26°F (−3°C). But just before noon, cold air moved in. Within a few hours, the temperature plunged to 0°F (−18°C), while the wind blew over 45 miles (72 km) per hour. Strong gusts dropped the windchill to −60°F (−51°C). The Blizzard of '77 had begun.

Snowy Record

The Blizzard of '77 sealed Buffalo's standing as one of the snowiest cities in the United States. Buffalo usually receives around 97 inches (246 cm) of snow per year. In 1977, Buffalo received 199.4 inches (506.5 cm) of snow. The winter of 1977 set a record for Buffalo that still stands.

car buried in snow

woman shovels her driveway during Blizzard of '77

◁ **This snow pile approached the height of a highway sign in Buffalo, New York, following the Blizzard of '77.**

19

snow removal after the Blizzard of '77

Many people needed more than a shovel to clear their driveways and uncover their cars after the Blizzard of '77. ▽

During the next few days, about 12 inches (30 cm) of new snow fell. However, the snow that had piled up on frozen Lake Erie continued to blow into Buffalo and the surrounding areas. Snowdrifts were so high that some houses were buried up to the roofs. Thousands of cars were abandoned in the streets, completely covered with snow. Blocked roads prevented snowplows from clearing the snow. Travel into and out of Buffalo was nearly impossible.

On the first day of February, the blizzard came to an end. Cleanup, however, continued throughout the rest of the month and cost over $20 million. Twenty-nine people lost their lives during the storm.

Digging Out

The Blizzard of '77 was the first blizzard in US history to be declared a national **disaster**. Over 500 people from the National Guard and about 300 army soldiers were part of the task force to clear snow and rescue people.

army vehicle moving snow after the Blizzard of '77

THE STORM OF THE CENTURY

In March 1993, three different storm systems combined in the Gulf of Mexico to create a giant storm that some people call the "Storm of the Century." For several days, snow fell as far south as Florida and as far north as Canada.

Over $6 billion in damage was caused by the blizzard. The damage could have been much worse, though. The NWS was able to **predict** the storm 5 days in advance and the blizzard conditions 2 days before. Over 100 million people were able to prepare for the storm before it struck.

New York City during the Storm of the Century

Widespread Damage

Birmingham, Alabama, a city that normally gets less than 2 inches (5 cm) of snow per year, received 13 inches (33 cm) of snow during the storm. The storm system also brought thunderstorms, floods, and windstorms to other parts of the country. As a result of the storm, a ship called the *Gold Bond Conveyor* sank in the Atlantic Ocean.

◁ The Storm of the Century helped change the way storms are forecast, or predicted. Afterwards, the NWS improved its methods of predicting storms as well as its ability to issue weather warnings.

23

PREDICTING BLIZZARDS

Today, computer programs are used to predict the path that a blizzard might take. These programs use facts gathered from **radar**, **satellites**, and weather balloons in order to create models of a storm system.

Radar was first used to spot aircraft during World War II. It's also useful when tracking the direction of a storm. Pictures taken by satellites can show a storm as it's forming as well as track its movement. Weather balloons take measurements of temperature, wind speed, and water vapor levels. When all of these methods are combined, forecasters can often predict when and where a blizzard will strike.

Room for Improvement

Computers were first used to forecast blizzards in the 1950s. Computer programs have improved, but they aren't foolproof. For instance, computer models predicted that Washington, DC, would receive less than 1 inch (2.5 cm) of snow on January 25, 2000. Instead, the city was hit by a blizzard that brought over 1 foot (30.5 cm) of snow.

This satellite picture shows the wide extent of a US storm system on January 31, 2011. Twenty states expected storms.

weather balloons

POWERFUL PUNCH

Even areas that know a blizzard is coming are often unprepared or unable to deal with the storm. From December 26 to December 27, 2010, a blizzard pounded the East Coast and left thousands of travelers across the country stuck. The storm caused airlines to cancel more than 7,000 flights. In New York City, passengers were trapped in subway cars for up to 9 hours.

Just over a month later, Chicago, Illinois, was hit with one of the worst blizzards it had seen in years. Although it had been predicted more than 2 days before it hit, the blizzard still managed to bring the city to a standstill.

cars abandoned in Chicago, Illinois, on
February 2, 2011

Both the 2010 blizzard in New York and the 2011 blizzard in Chicago featured a rare type of snowstorm called thundersnow. Thundersnow is a storm in which thunder and lightning are accompanied by heavy snow instead of rain.

△ Airplanes get special treatment during snowstorms. Special chemicals are sprayed on them to take ice off their wings and body. Other chemicals prevent ice from forming.

PREPARING FOR A BLIZZARD

If a person is caught in a blizzard, the most important thing they can do is find shelter and stay dry. Hypothermia and frostbite can occur very quickly if a person gets wet in the cold. During winter, it's a good idea to keep blankets, flashlights, and snacks in the car in case the car gets stuck.

Since blizzards can cause homes to lose power and heat, it's also a good idea to keep your house stocked with flashlights, a battery-powered radio, and foods that don't need to be cooked. When it comes to blizzards, you can never be too prepared.

Another Snowy Danger

A person who's stuck outdoors during a blizzard and is hungry or thirsty may become tempted to eat snow. Eating snow is dangerous because it will lower body temperature. This could lead to hypothermia. If possible, the snow should be melted first.

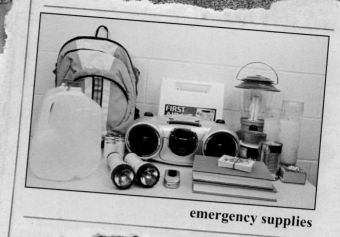
emergency supplies

◁ It's important for drivers to go slowly on streets during a storm. In addition, special tires can make driving safer.

GLOSSARY

damage: harm. Also, to cause harm.

disaster: an event that causes great loss, damage, hardship, unhappiness, or death

extreme: great or severe

gust: a sudden, powerful rush of wind

hurricane: a severe storm with rain and strong winds

predict: to guess what will happen in the future based on facts or knowledge

radar: a system that uses radio waves to find the location and speed of objects

satellite: an object that circles Earth in order to collect and send information or aid in communication

snowdrift: a mound of snow created by wind

telegraph: a method of communicating using electric signals sent through wires

water vapor: water in the form of gas

whiteout: a condition in which falling or blowing snow makes visibility very poor

FOR MORE INFORMATION

Books

Fleisher, Paul. *Lightning, Hurricanes, and Blizzards: The Science of Storms.* Minneapolis, MN: Lerner Publications, 2011.

Hardyman, Robyn. *Snow and Blizzards.* New York, NY: PowerKids Press, 2010.

Markovics, Joyce. *Blitzed by a Blizzard!* New York, NY: Bearport Publishing, 2010.

Websites

FEMA for Kids
www.fema.gov/kids/
Read how to prepare for severe weather and many types of disasters.

Science of a Blizzard
www.history.com/videos/science-of-a-blizzard#science-of-a-blizzard
Watch a video to learn more about the science of a blizzard.

The Weather Channel Kids!
www.theweatherchannelkids.com
Learn about different types of weather while watching videos and playing games.

INDEX